A YEAR OF STORMS

A YEAR OF STORMS

A COLLECTION OF POETRY AND SHORT STORIES

Compiled by Melinda Frank, Alexa Horn,
Brianna Patterson, and Madison Schmidt

EMPIRE PRESS

ISBN 978-1-60962-118-6

Melinda Frank, marketing director; Alexa Horn, designer;
Brianna Patterson, acquisitions editor; and Madison Schmidt,
copyeditor.

Printed by UNL Printing

E-version available at empirepress1.wixsite.com/empirepress1.

CONTENTS

INTRODUCTION

I n one year, about ten hurricanes occur, over one
thousand tornadoes form, and over 16 million
thunderstorms strike the earth. Storms can be interpreted
as more than just rain or snow; they are emotions,
relationships, and reflections of the innermost thoughts
of humans. Storms help make sense of the turmoils life
can bring. Storms change throughout the year with the
people who experience them. This anthology takes readers
through a year of storms and some of literature's most
profound authors such as Madison Cawein, Algernon
Blackwood, Emily Dickinson, and Emily Brontë, to name
a few. They have experienced storms, felt storms, and
captured those storms on the page.

The anthology begins with the season of Fall. After
the dry spell most summers bring, the first rainfall is
representative of the start of a new season. This section
opens with an excerpt from the short story, "The Rain
Cloud" by an anonymous writer. This story was selected
due to its deep descriptions of rain, and its presence in
all four seasons, with a first appearance in fall. Madison
Cawein contributed two poems to this section titled

"Before the Rain" and "After Rain". The atmosphere before and after a rainstorm is so present to the observer, in this case the reader, so that time is a part of thes storm itself. Nature is a prevalent theme during fall storms. Anne Brontë's poem "Lines Composed in a Wood on a Windy Day," is featured in this section and weaves the storm, the sea, the wind, and the forest so that they appear to be acting as one.

As the weather becomes colder, the light sprinkles of fall turn into snow and wind. The winter section begins with Algernon Blackwood's story titled "The Glamour of the Snow," describing a man's encounter with snow personified. The section includes poets Ralph Waldo Emerson and Robert Frost who center their work around a life experience while using snow as a metaphorical object for concealing. An author biography is written in this section for Ralph Waldo Emerson who uses snow in his poem for privacy with a family, keeping the regular disturbances of friends shut out.

After the snow melts, rain showers come again in spring with the promise of abundant nature and life that is to come. The spring contains autobiographies of popular writers Emily Dickinson, Hans Christian Anderson and Edgar Allan Poe. The section opens with Hans Christian Anderson's short story, "The Storm Shakes the Shield." The privacy created with winter snow is destroyed with the spring storm. The narrator tells the story of his grandfather's past when a massive storm hits a small town. The busiest time of year for thunderstorms and the inspirations that come with them, the spring section is the longest section of the anthology.

As rainfalls become few and far between, a dry

season usually strikes during the summer, but not in this anthology. The summer section begins with a short story titled "Summer Snowstorm" by Adam Chase. The story is centered around a man named Johnny Sloman who predicts snow in July. Due to the unlikely event, people are intrigued when they discover that all of his weather predictions come true. The short story is followed with a poem by Emily Brontë, and then several more poems centered around the storms of summer. When long days of heat are broken by storms, there is an air of unpredictableness, therefore the poems in this section have a theme of wild storms and their effect on the writer.

With the millions of storms that form and penetrate the atmosphere every year, it is a wonder the world is not in disarray and abandonment. It is the people who experience the storms that react to the aftermath and find the beauty. Sometimes the storms do not leave destruction at all, but only the feeling of having experienced something wild and natural.

FALL

THE RAIN CLOUD
EXCERPTS FROM CHAPTER I

ANONYMOUS

Every season has its own peculiar rains. What can be more refreshing or invigorating than the showers of spring? When the snows of February have disappeared, and the blustering winds of March have performed their office of drying up the excess of moisture, and preparing the earth for fruitfulness, and when the young buds and blossoms of April are peeping forth beneath the influence of the sun, and the trees and hedges are attired in their new robes of tender green, how soon would all this beauty languish but for the showers of spring! Several dry days, perhaps, have passed, and the wreaths of dust which are raised by the wind show that the earth wants moisture; but before a drop falls there is a general lull throughout all nature; not a leaf is heard to rustle; the birds are mute and the cattle stand in expectation of the refreshing fall. At last the pools and rivulets are "dimpled" by a few soft drops, the forerunners of the general shower. And this shower, unlike the heavier rains of summer, comes stealing on so gently, that the tinkling sound of its fall is heard among the branches of the bursting trees long before it is felt by those who walk beneath their slight shelter.

Rapidly does the landscape brighten under the influence of the welcome shower; and as it becomes more rich and extensive, all nature seems to rise up and rejoice. The birds chirp merrily among the foliage; the flowers raise their drooping heads, and the thirsty ground drinks in with eager haste the mellowing rains. All day long, perhaps, does the rain continue to fall, until the earth is fully moistened and "enriched with vegetable life." At length, towards evening, the sun peeps out from among the broken clouds, and lights up, by his sudden radiance, the lovely scene. Myriads of rain-drops sparkle like gems beneath his beams; a soft mist that seems to mingle earth and sky gradually rolls away, and "moist, and bright, and green, the landscape laughs around." Now pours forth the evening concert from the woods, while warbling brooks, and lowing herds, appear to answer to the sound. Such are some of the delightful effects of spring-showers.

...

If rain is not at all seasons pleasant and delightful, neither are rain-clouds among the most beautiful which diversify the landscape of the sky; for it has been well remarked, that "all the fine-weather clouds are beautiful, and those connected with rain and wind mostly the reverse." What, indeed, can be more striking than the aërial landscapes of fine weather, in which, by an easy fancy, we can trace trees and towers, magnificent ruins and glaciers, natural bridges and palaces, all dashed with torrents of light or frowning in shadow, glowing like burnished silver, glittering in a golden light, or melting into the most enchanting hues? But with all this beauty the eye is seldom capable of judging correctly of the proper size and forms and motions of clouds. The same cloud which

to one observer may be glowing with light, to another
may be enveloped in shadow. That which appears to be its
summit may be only a portion of its outer edge, while that
which seems to be its lower bed may really be a portion
of its further border. A spectator, on the summit of a
tall cliff, may observe what he takes to be a single cloud;
while a second spectator, on lower ground, will perceive
that there are two clouds. The motions of clouds are so
deceptive, that they often seem to be moving in a curve
over the great concave of heaven, while they are in fact
advancing in nearly a right line. Suppose, for example that
a cloud is moving from the distant horizon towards the
place where we stand, in a uniform horizontal line without
changing either in size or form. Such a cloud, when first
seen, will appear to be in contact with the distant horizon,
and consequently much nearer to us than it really is. As it
advances towards us, it will seem to rise into the sky, and
to become gradually larger till it is almost directly overhead.
Continuing its progress, it will then seem again to descend
and to lessen in size as gradually as it had before increased;
till at length it disappears in the distant horizon at a point
exactly opposite to that at which it was first seen. Thus the
same cloud, without varying its motion in the least from
a straight line, and remaining throughout of the same
size and form, would seem to be continually varying in
magnitude; and the line of its motion, instead of being
straight, would appear to be curved. This is one of the
most simple cases that can be supposed: but the clouds as
they exist in nature do not remain of the same magnitude,
but are constantly changing in form, in size, in direction,
and in velocity; so that it is quite impossible to form an
accurate idea of their shape and size, or to explain their

motions. Clouds, at different elevations, may often be seen to move in different directions under the influence of different currents of wind.

LINES COMPOSED IN A
WOOD ON A WINDY DAY
ANNE BRONTË

My soul is awakened, my spirit is soaring
And carried aloft on the winds of the breeze;
For above and around me the wild wind is roaring,
Arousing to rapture the earth and the seas.

The long withered grass in the sunshine is glancing,
The bare trees are tossing their branches on high;
The dead leaves beneath them are merrily dancing,
The white clouds are scudding across the blue sky.

I wish I could see how the ocean is lashing
The foam of its billows to whirlwinds of spray;
I wish I could see how its proud waves are dashing,
And hear the wild roar of their thunder to-day!

RAIN
EDWARD THOMAS

Rain, midnight rain, nothing but the wild rain
On this bleak hut, and solitude, and me
Remembering again that I shall die
And neither hear the rain nor give it thanks
For washing me cleaner than I have been
Since I was born into solitude.
Blessed are the dead that the rain rains upon:
But here I pray that none whom once I loved
Is dying tonight or lying still awake
Solitary, listening to the rain,
Either in pain or thus in sympathy
Helpless among the living and the dead,
Like a cold water among broken reeds,
Myriads of broken reeds all still and stiff,
Like me who have no love which this wild rain
Has not dissolved except the love of death,
If love it be towards what is perfect and
Cannot, the tempest tells me, disappoint.

MADISON CAWEIN

Born on March 23, 1865, Madison Julius Cawein was an American poet from Louisville, Kentucky. As the son of a medicine man, Cawein fell in love with nature. He worked as a pool hall cashier for at least six years until he was able to save enough money to stay at home and write. Madison Cawein was very successful as a poet and was able to make a happy living off his poems alone. He died on December 8, 1914 after being placed on the Author Club of New York City's relief list.

He was known to write of nature, instead of humanity, though many found this strange. Most of his work reflected his home state of Kentucky. Cawein was influenced by poets like Percy Bysshe Shelley and John Keats. He was even known as the "Keats of Kentucky." He wrote 1,500 poems and 36 books. Cawein published his first book in 1887. His poems expressed his deep love for nature, English and European literature, and even mythology. Cawein published one of his last poems titled "Waste Land" a year before his death in a Chicago magazine, which scholars believe had inspired T.S. Eliot, another famous poet, to write "The Waste Land" which was published in 1922.

BEFORE THE RAIN

MADISON CAWEIN

Before the rain, low in the obscure east,
Weak and morose the moon hung, sickly gray;
Around its disc the storm mists, cracked and creased,
Wove an enormous web, wherein it lay
Like some white spider hungry for its prey.
Vindictive looked the scowling firmament,
In which each star, that flashed a dagger ray,
Seemed filled with malice of some dark intent.
The marsh-frog croaked; and underneath the stone
The peevish cricket raised a creaking cry.

Within the world these sounds were heard alone,
Save when the ruffian wind swept from the sky,
Making each tree like some sad spirit sigh;
Or shook the clumsy beetle from its weed,
That, in the drowsy darkness, bungling by,
Sharded the silence with its feverish speed.

Slowly the tempest gathered. Hours passed
Before was heard the thunder's sullen drum
Rumbling night's hollow; and the Earth at last,

Restless with waiting,—like a woman, dumb
With doubting of the love that should have clomb
Her casement hours ago,—avowed again,
'Mid protestations, joy that he had come.
And all night long I heard the Heavens explain.

AFTER RAIN
MADISON CAWEIN

Behold the blossom-bosomed Day again,
With all the star-white Hours in her train,
Laughs out of pearl-lights through a golden ray,
That, leaning on the woodland wildness, blends
A sprinkled amber with the showers that lay
Their oblong emeralds on the leafy ends.
Behold her bend with maiden-braided brows
Above the wildflower, sidewise with its strain
Of dewy happiness, to kiss again
Each drop to death; or, under rainy boughs,
With fingers, fragrant as the woodland rain,
Gather the sparkles from the sycamore,
To set within the core
Of crimson roses girdling her hips,
Where each bud dreams and drips.

Smoothing her blue-black hair,—where many a tusk
Of iris flashes,—like the falchions keen
Of Faery round blue banners of their Queen,—
Is it a Naiad singing in the dusk,
That haunts the spring, where all the moss is musk

With footsteps of the flowers on the banks?
Or but a wild-bird voluble with thanks?

Balm for each blade of grass: the Hours prepare
A festival each weed's invited to.
Each bee is drunken with the honied air:
And all the heaven is eloquent with blue.
The wet hay glitters, and the harvester
Tinkles his scythe,—as twinkling as the dew,—
That shall not spare
Blossom or brier in its sweeping path;
And, ere it cut one swath,
Rings them they die, and tells them to prepare.

What is the spice that haunts each glen and glade?
A Dryad's lips, who slumbers in the shade?
A Faun, who lets the heavy ivy-wreath
Slip to his thigh as, reaching up, he pulls
The chestnut blossoms in whole bosomfuls?
A sylvan Spirit, whose sweet mouth doth breathe
Her viewless presence near us, unafraid?
Or troops of ghosts of blooms, that whitely wade
The brook? whose wisdom knows no other song
But that the bird sings where it builds beneath
The wild-rose and sits singing all day long.

Oh, let me sit with silence for a space,
A little while forgetting that fierce part
Of man that struggles in the toiling mart;
Where God can look into my heart's own heart
From unsoiled heights made amiable with grace;
And where the sermons that the old oaks keep

Can steal into me.—And what better then
Than, turning to the moss a quiet face,
To fall asleep? a little while to sleep
And dream of wiser worlds and wiser men.

WINTER

ALGERNON BLACKWOOD

Algernon Blackwood was born in Shooter's Hill, Kent on March 14, 1869. He grew up in a strict Calvinist family and attended private school. One of his teachers introduced him to therapeutic hypnotism and Blackwood decided to study psychiatric medicine. He studied at the Moravian Brotherhood school in Germany, Wellington College in Cambridge, and the University of Edinburgh in the United Kingdom but gave up the medicine practice. He attempted a dairy farm and hotel business in Canada but neither suited him. After working as a reporter in New York during the 1890s, Blackwood returned to England and began to write. He participated in World War I as British military intelligence. Algernon Blackwood died December 10, 1951 after undergoing a series of strokes.

Blackwood was known for writing stories of the supernatural, with his works landing in the Gothic genre and often being categorized as "weird fiction". Admirer and fellow writer H. P. Lovecraft praised Blackwood's most arguably famous work, "The Willows" as the best "weird tale" of all time. The story, featuring two friends canoeing down the Danube river, meeting the fierce willows to complicate their journey, gives the "spiritual terror" that Blackwood aimed to include in all of his works. The short story included in this anthology comes from a collection published by Macmillan in 1912. The collection, titled Pan's Garden: A Volume of Nature Stories, pulls from Blackwood's time spent in the Canadian backwoods the summer after his hotel business failed in 1892. Chilling winds often appear in Blackwood's writing, submerging the reader, just as in "The Glamour of the Snow".

THE GLAMOUR OF THE SNOW
EXCERPTS FROM SECTIONS I, VI, AND VII

ALGERNON BLACKWOOD

I

Hibbert, always conscious of two worlds, was in this mountain village conscious of three. It lay on the slopes of the Valais Alps, and he had taken a room in the little post office, where he could be at peace to write his book, yet at the same time enjoy the winter sports and find companionship in the hotels when he wanted it.

The three worlds that met and mingled here seemed to his imaginative temperament very obvious, though it is doubtful if another mind less intuitively equipped would have seen them so well-defined. There was the world of tourist English, civilised, quasi-educated, to which he belonged by birth, at any rate; there was the world of peasants to which he felt himself drawn by sympathy—for he loved and admired their toiling, simple life; and there was this other—which he could only call the world of Nature. To this last, however, in virtue of a vehement poetic imagination, and a tumultuous pagan instinct fed by his very blood, he felt that most of him belonged. The others borrowed from it, as it were, for visits. Here, with the soul of Nature, hid his central life.

Between all three was conflict—potential conflict. On the skating-rink each Sunday the tourists regarded the natives as intruders; in the church the peasants plainly questioned: "Why do you come? We are here to worship; you to stare and whisper!" For neither of these two worlds accepted the other. And neither did Nature accept the tourists, for it took advantage of their least mistakes, and indeed, even of the peasant-world "accepted" only those who were strong and bold enough to invade her savage domain with sufficient skill to protect themselves from several forms of—death.

Now Hibbert was keenly aware of this potential conflict and want of harmony; he felt outside, yet caught by it—torn in the three directions because he was partly of each world, but wholly in only one. There grew in him a constant, subtle effort—or, at least, desire—to unify them and decide positively to which he should belong and live in. The attempt, of course, was largely subconscious. It was the natural instinct of a richly imaginative nature seeking the point of equilibrium, so that the mind could feel at peace and his brain be free to do good work.

Among the guests no one especially claimed his interest. The men were nice but undistinguished—athletic schoolmasters, doctors snatching a holiday, good fellows all; the women, equally various—the clever, the would-be-fast, the dare-to-be-dull, the women "who understood," and the usual pack of jolly dancing girls and "flappers." And Hibbert, with his forty odd years of thick experience behind him, got on well with the lot; he understood them all; they belonged to definite, predigested types that are the same the world over, and that he had met the world over long ago.

But to none of them did he belong. His nature was too "multiple" to subscribe to the set of shibboleths of any one class. And, since all liked him, and felt that somehow he seemed outside of them—spectator, looker-on—all sought to claim him.

In a sense, therefore, the three worlds fought for him: natives, tourists, Nature....

It was thus began the singular conflict for the soul of Hibbert. In his own soul, however, it took place. Neither the peasants nor the tourists were conscious that they fought for anything. And Nature, they say, is merely blind and automatic.

The assault upon him of the peasants may be left out of account, for it is obvious that they stood no chance of success. The tourist world, however, made a gallant effort to subdue him to themselves. But the evenings in the hotel, when dancing was not in order, were—English. The provincial imagination was set upon a throne and worshipped heavily through incense of the stupidest conventions possible. Hibbert used to go back early to his room in the post office to work.

"It is a mistake on my part to have realised that there is any conflict at all," he thought, as he crunched home over the snow at midnight after one of the dances. "It would have been better to have kept outside it all and done my work. Better," he added, looking back down the silent village street to the church tower, "and—safer."

The adjective slipped from his mind before he was aware of it. He turned with an involuntary start and looked about him. He knew perfectly well what it meant—this thought that had thrust its head up from the instinctive region. He understood, without being able to express it fully, the meaning that betrayed itself in the choice of the adjective. For if he had ignored the existence of this conflict he would at the same time, have remained outside the arena. Whereas now he had entered the lists. Now this battle for his soul must have issue. And he knew that the spell of Nature was greater for him than all other spells in the world combined—greater than love, revelry, pleasure, greater even than study. He had always been afraid to let himself go. His pagan soul dreaded her terrific powers of witchery even while he worshipped.

The little village already slept. The world lay smothered in snow. The châlet roofs shone white beneath the moon, and pitch-black shadows gathered against the walls of the church. His eye rested a moment on the square stone tower with its frosted cross that pointed to the sky: then travelled with a leap of many thousand feet to the enormous mountains that brushed the brilliant stars. Like a forest rose the huge peaks above the slumbering village, measuring the night and heavens. They beckoned him. And something born of the snowy desolation, born of the midnight and the silent grandeur, born of the great listening hollows of the night, something that lay 'twixt terror and wonder, dropped from the vast wintry spaces down into his heart— and called him. Very softly, unrecorded in any word or thought his brain could compass, it laid its spell upon him. Fingers of snow brushed the surface of his heart. The power and quiet majesty of the winter's night appalled him....

Fumbling a moment with the big unwieldy key, he let himself in and went upstairs to bed. Two thoughts went with him—apparently quite ordinary and sensible ones:

"What fools these peasants are to sleep through such a

night!" And the other:

"Those dances tire me. I'll never go again. My work only suffers in the morning." The claims of peasants and tourists upon him seemed thus in a single instant weakened.

The clash of battle troubled half his dreams. Nature had sent her Beauty of the Night and won the first assault. The others, routed and dismayed, fled far away.

VI

And at once into his mind passed the hush and softness of the snow—yet with it a searching, crying wildness for the heights. He knew by some incalculable, swift instinct she would not meet him in the village street. It was not there, amid crowding houses, she would speak to him. Indeed, already she had disappeared, melted from view up the white vista of the moonlit road. Yonder, he divined, she waited where the highway narrowed abruptly into the mountain path beyond the châlets.

It did not even occur to him to hesitate; mad though it seemed, and was—this sudden craving for the heights with her, at least for open spaces where the snow lay thick and fresh—it was too imperious to be denied. He does not remember going up to his room, putting the sweater over his evening clothes, and getting into the fur gauntlet gloves and the helmet cap of wool. Most certainly he has no recollection of fastening on his ski; he must have done it automatically. Some faculty of normal observation was in abeyance, as it were. His mind was out beyond the village— out with the snowy mountains and the moon.

Henri Défago, putting up the shutters over his café windows, saw him pass, and wondered mildly: "Un monsieur qui fait du ski à cette heure! Il est Anglais, done

...!" He shrugged his shoulders, as though a man had the right to choose his own way of death. And Marthe Perotti, the hunchback wife of the shoemaker, looking by chance from her window, caught his figure moving swiftly up the road. She had other thoughts, for she knew and believed the old traditions of the witches and snow-beings that steal the souls of men. She had even heard, 'twas said, the dreaded "synagogue" pass roaring down the street at night, and now, as then, she hid her eyes. "They've called to him ... and he must go," she murmured, making the sign of the cross.

But no one sought to stop him. Hibbert recalls only a single incident until he found himself beyond the houses, searching for her along the fringe of forest where the moonlight met the snow in a bewildering frieze of fantastic shadows. And the incident was simply this—that he remembered passing the church. Catching the outline of its tower against the stars, he was aware of a faint sense of hesitation. A vague uneasiness came and went—jarred unpleasantly across the flow of his excited feelings, chilling exhilaration. He caught the instant's discord, dismissed it, and—passed on. The seduction of the snow smothered the hint before he realised that it had brushed the skirts of warning.

And then he saw her. She stood there waiting in a little clear space of shining snow, dressed all in white, part of the moonlight and the glistening background, her slender figure just discernible.

"I waited, for I knew you would come," the silvery little voice of windy beauty floated down to him. "You had to come."

"I'm ready," he answered, "I knew it too."

The world of Nature caught him to its heart in those few words—the wonder and the glory of the night and snow. Life leaped within him. The passion of his pagan soul exulted, rose in joy, flowed out to her. He neither reflected nor considered, but let himself go like the veriest schoolboy in the wildness of first love.

"Give me your hand," he cried, "I'm coming ...!"

"A little farther on, a little higher," came her delicious answer. "Here it is too near the village—and the church."

And the words seemed wholly right and natural; he did not dream of questioning them; he understood that, with this little touch of civilisation in sight, the familiarity he suggested was impossible. Once out upon the open mountains, 'mid the freedom of huge slopes and towering peaks, the stars and moon to witness and the wilderness of snow to watch, they could taste an innocence of happy intercourse free from the dead conventions that imprison literal minds.

He urged his pace, yet did not quite overtake her. The girl kept always just a little bit ahead of his best efforts.... And soon they left the trees behind and passed on to the enormous slopes of the sea of snow that rolled in mountainous terror and beauty to the stars. The wonder of the white world caught him away. Under the steady moonlight it was more than haunting. It was a living, white, bewildering power that deliciously confused the senses and laid a spell of wild perplexity upon the heart. It was a personality that cloaked, and yet revealed, itself through all this sheeted whiteness of snow. It rose, went with him, fled before, and followed after. Slowly it dropped lithe, gleaming arms about his neck, gathering him in....

Certainly some soft persuasion coaxed his very soul,

urging him ever forwards, upwards, on towards the higher
icy slopes. Judgment and reason left their throne, it seemed,
completely, as in the madness of intoxication. The girl, slim
and seductive, kept always just ahead, so that he never quite
came up with her. He saw the white enchantment of her
face and figure, something that streamed about her neck
flying like a wreath of snow in the wind, and heard the
alluring accents of her whispering voice that called from
time to time: "A little farther on, a little higher.... Then we'll
run home together!"

Sometimes he saw her hand stretched out to find his
own, but each time, just as he came up with her, he saw
her still in front, the hand and arm withdrawn. They took
a gentle angle of ascent. The toil seemed nothing. In this
crystal, wine-like air fatigue vanished. The sishing of the
ski through the powdery surface of the snow was the only
sound that broke the stillness; this, with his breathing and
the rustle of her skirts, was all he heard. Cold moonshine,
snow, and silence held the world. The sky was black, and
the peaks beyond cut into it like frosted wedges of iron
and steel. Far below the valley slept, the village long since
hidden out of sight. He felt that he could never tire.... The
sound of the church clock rose from time to time faintly
through the air—more and more distant.

"Give me your hand. It's time now to turn back."

"Just one more slope," she laughed. "That ridge above
us. Then we'll make for home." And her low voice mingled
pleasantly with the purring of their ski. His own seemed
harsh and ugly by comparison.

"But I have never come so high before. It's glorious!
This world of silent snow and moonlight—and you. You're
a child of the snow, I swear. Let me come up—closer—to

see your face—and touch your little hand."

Her laughter answered him.

"Come on! A little higher. Here we're quite alone together."

"It's magnificent," he cried. "But why did you hide away so long? I've looked and searched for you in vain ever since we skated—" he was going to say "ten days ago," but the accurate memory of time had gone from him; he was not sure whether it was days or years or minutes. His thoughts of earth were scattered and confused.

"You looked for me in the wrong places," he heard her murmur just above him. "You looked in places where I never go. Hotels and houses kill me. I avoid them." She laughed—a fine, shrill, windy little laugh.

"I loathe them too—"

He stopped. The girl had suddenly come quite close. A breath of ice passed through his very soul. She had touched him.

"But this awful cold!" he cried out, sharply, "this freezing cold that takes me. The wind is rising; it's a wind of ice. Come, let us turn ...!"

But when he plunged forward to hold her, or at least to look, the girl was gone again. And something in the way she stood there a few feet beyond, and stared down into his eyes so steadfastly in silence, made him shiver. The moonlight was behind her, but in some odd way he could not focus sight upon her face, although so close. The gleam of eyes he caught, but all the rest seemed white and snowy as though he looked beyond her—out into space....

The sound of the church bell came up faintly from the valley far below, and he counted the strokes—five. A sudden, curious weakness seized him as he listened. Deep within it was, deadly yet somehow sweet, and hard to resist. He felt like sinking down upon the snow and lying there.... They had been climbing for five hours.... It was, of course, the warning of complete exhaustion.

With a great effort he fought and overcame it. It passed away as suddenly as it came.

"We'll turn," he said with a decision he hardly felt. "It will be dawn before we reach the village again. Come at once. It's time for home."

The sense of exhilaration had utterly left him. An emotion that was akin to fear swept coldly through him. But her whispering answer turned it instantly to terror—a terror that gripped him horribly and turned him weak and unresisting.

"Our home is—here!" A burst of wild, high laughter, loud and shrill, accompanied the words. It was like a whistling wind. The wind had risen, and clouds obscured the moon. "A little higher—where we cannot hear the wicked bells," she cried, and for the first time seized him deliberately by the hand. She moved, was suddenly close against his face. Again she touched him.

And Hibbert tried to turn away in escape, and so trying, found for the first time that the power of the snow—that other power which does not exhilarate but deadens effort—was upon him. The suffocating weakness that it brings to exhausted men, luring them to the sleep of death in her clinging soft embrace, lulling the will and conquering all desire for life—this was awfully upon him. His feet were heavy and entangled. He could not turn or move.

The girl stood in front of him, very near; he felt her chilly breath upon his cheeks; her hair passed blindingly across his eyes; and that icy wind came with her. He saw her whiteness close; again, it seemed, his sight passed through her into space as though she had no face. Her arms were round his neck. She drew him softly downwards to his knees. He sank; he yielded utterly; he obeyed. Her weight was upon him, smothering, delicious. The snow was to his waist.... She kissed him softly on the lips, the eyes, all over his face. And then she spoke his name in that voice of love and wonder, the voice that held the accent of two others—both taken over long ago by Death—the voice of his mother, and of the woman he had loved.

He made one more feeble effort to resist. Then, realising even while he struggled that this soft weight about his heart was sweeter than anything life could ever bring, he let his muscles relax, and sank back into the soft oblivion of the covering snow. Her wintry kisses bore him into sleep.

VII

They say that men who know the sleep of exhaustion in the snow find no awakening on the hither side of death.... The hours passed and the moon sank down below the white world's rim. Then, suddenly, there came a little crash upon his breast and neck, and Hibbert—woke.

He slowly turned bewildered, heavy eyes upon the desolate mountains, stared dizzily about him, tried to rise. At first his muscles would not act; a numbing, aching pain possessed him. He uttered a long, thin cry for help, and heard its faintness swallowed by the wind. And then he understood vaguely why he was only warm—not dead. For this very wind that took his cry had built up a sheltering mound of driven snow against his body while he slept. Like a curving wave it ran beside him. It was the breaking of its over-toppling edge that caused the crash, and the coldness of the mass against his neck that woke him.

Dawn kissed the eastern sky; pale gleams of gold shot every peak with splendour; but ice was in the air, and the dry and frozen snow blew like powder from the surface of the slopes. He saw the points of his ski projecting just below him. Then he—remembered. It seems he had just strength enough to realise that, could he but rise and stand, he might fly with terrific impetus towards the woods and village far beneath. The ski would carry him. But if he failed and fell ...!

How he contrived it Hibbert never knew; this fear of death somehow called out his whole available reserve force. He rose slowly, balanced a moment, then, taking the angle of an immense zigzag, started down the awful slopes like an arrow from a bow. And automatically the splendid muscles of the practised ski-er and athlete saved and guided him, for he was hardly conscious of controlling either speed or direction. The snow stung face and eyes like fine steel shot; ridge after ridge flew past; the summits raced across the sky; the valley leaped up with bounds to meet him. He scarcely felt the ground beneath his feet as the huge slopes and distance melted before the lightning speed of that descent from death to life.

He took it in four mile-long zigzags, and it was the turning at each corner that nearly finished him, for then the strain of balancing taxed to the verge of collapse the remnants of his strength.

Slopes that have taken hours to climb can be descended in a short half-hour on ski, but Hibbert had lost all count of time. Quite other thoughts and feelings mastered him in that wild, swift dropping through the air that was like the flight of a bird. For ever close upon his heels came following forms and voices with the whirling snow-dust. He heard that little silvery voice of death and laughter at his back. Shrill and wild, with the whistling of the wind past his ears, he caught its pursuing tones; but in anger now, no longer soft and coaxing. And it was accompanied; she did not follow alone. It seemed a host of these flying figures of the snow chased madly just behind him. He felt them furiously smite his neck and cheeks, snatch at his hands and try to entangle his feet and ski in drifts. His eyes they blinded, and they caught his breath away.

The terror of the heights and snow and winter desolation urged him forward in the maddest race with death a human being ever knew; and so terrific was the speed that before the gold and crimson had left the summits to touch the ice-lips of the lower glaciers, he saw the friendly forest far beneath swing up and welcome him.

And it was then, moving slowly along the edge of the woods, he saw a light. A man was carrying it. A procession of human figures was passing in a dark line laboriously through the snow. And—he heard the sound of chanting.

Instinctively, without a second's hesitation, he changed his course. No longer flying at an angle as before, he pointed his ski straight down the mountain-side. The dreadful steepness did not frighten him. He knew full well it meant a crashing tumble at the bottom, but he also knew it meant a doubling of his speed—with safety at the end. For, though no definite thought passed through his mind, he understood that it was the village curé who carried that little gleaming lantern in the dawn, and that he was taking the Host to a châlet on the lower slopes—to some peasant in extremis. He remembered her terror of the church and bells. She feared the holy symbols.

There was one last wild cry in his ears as he started, a shriek of the wind before his face, and a rush of stinging snow against closed eyelids—and then he dropped through empty space. Speed took sight from him. It seemed he flew off the surface of the world.

THE SNOWSTORM
JAMES THOMSON

Through the hushed air the whitening shower descends,
At first thin wavering; till at last the flakes
Fall broad and wide and fast, dimming the day,
With a continual flow. The cherished fields
Put on their winter robe of purest white.
'Tis brightness all: save where the new snow melts
Along the mazy current.
Low the woods
Bow their hoar head; and ere the languid sun
Faint from the west emits its evening ray,
Earth's universal face, deep-hid and chill,
Is one wild dazzling waste, that buries wide
The works of man.
Drooping, the laborer ox
Stands covered o'er with snow, and then demands
The fruit of all his toil. The fowls of heaven,
Tamed by the cruel season, crowd around
The winnowing store, and claim the little boon
Which Providence assigns them.
One alone,
The Redbreast, sacred to the household gods,

Wisely regardful of the embroiling sky,
In joyless fields and thorny thickets leaves
His shivering mates, and pays to trusted man
His annual visit.
Half-afraid, he first
Against the window beats; then, brisk, alights
On the warm hearth; then, hopping o'er the floor,
Eyes all the smiling family askance,
And pecks, and starts, and wonders where he is;
Till, more familiar grown, the table crumbs
Attract his slender feet.
The foodless wilds
Pour forth their brown inhabitants. The hare,
Though timorous of heart, and hard beset
By death in various forms, dark snares and dogs,
And more unpitying men, the garden seeks,
Urged on by fearless want. The bleating kind.
Eye the bleak heaven, and next the glistening earth,
With looks of dumb despair; then, sad dispersed,
Dig for the withered herb through heaps of snow
Now, shepherds, to your helpless charge be kind,
Baffle the raging year, and fill their pens
With food at will; lodge them below the storm,
And watch them strict; for from the bellowing east,
In this dire season, oft the whirlwind's wing
Sweeps up the burden of whole wintry plains
In one wide waft, and o'er the hapless flocks,
Hid in the hollow of two neighboring hills,
The billowy tempest 'whelms; till, upward urged,
The valley to a shining mountain swells,
Tipped with a wreath high-curling in the sky

TO WINTER

WILLIAM BLAKE

O Winter! bar thine adamantine doors:
The north is thine; there hast thou built thy dark
Deep-founded habitation. Shake not thy roofs
Nor bend thy pillars with thine iron car.

He hears me not, but o'er the yawning deep
Rides heavy; his storms are unchain'd, sheathed
In ribbed steel; I dare not lift mine eyes;
For he hath rear'd his scepter o'er the world.

Lo! now the direful monster, whose skin clings
To his strong bones, strides o'er the groaning rocks:
He withers all in silence, and in his hand
Unclothes the earth, and freezes up frail life.

He takes his seat upon the cliffs, the mariner
Cries in vain. Poor little wretch! that deal'st
With storms; till heaven smiles, and the monster
Is driven yelling to his caves beneath Mount Hecla.

RALPH WALDO EMERSON

    Ralph Waldo Emerson was born on May 25, 1803 in Boston, Massachusetts. Known as a poet, Emerson was also an essayist, lecturer, and a leader of the transcendentalist movement. Emerson attended Harvard College, the undergraduate liberal arts school at Harvard University, where he was the freshman messenger for the president. Emerson seemed to work many jobs throughout his academic career in order to pay for tuition. After graduating, Emerson traveled to help teach at his mother's women's school. Emerson then found a passion in preaching and began working in the ministry, eventually found that he did not want to become a priest in 1831, and thereafter pursued his writing. Ralph Waldo Emerson eventually died of pneumonia on April 27, 1882.

    When he was 18, he was his Class Poet at Harvard University and presented an original poem on Harvard's Class Day. Emerson's first published book was titled Nature and was written after he had left the ministry and became a part of the transcendentalist movement. This movement challenged the ideas of the church, but Emerson fully believed them and even went on to edit the Transcendentalist journal. As Emerson moved further away from the church, people became more shocked with his writing and involvement in the transcendentalist movement. Emerson published extremely scholarly work as well that helped to tie cultures together in a new way.

THE SNOW STORM
RALPH WALDO EMERSON

Announced by all the trumpets of the sky,
Arrives the snow, and, driving o'er the fields,
Seems nowhere to alight: the whited air
Hides hills and woods, the river, and the heaven,
And veils the farmhouse at the garden's end.
The sled and traveler stopped, the courier's feet
Delayed, all friends shut out, the housemates sit
Around the radiant fireplace, enclosed
In a tumultuous privacy of storm.

Come see the north wind's masonry.
Out of an unseen quarry evermore
Furnished with tile, the fierce artificer
Curves his white bastions with projected roof
Round every windward stake, or tree, or door.
Speeding, the myriad-handed, his wild work
So fanciful, so savage, nought cares he
For number or proportion. Mockingly,
On coop or kennel he hangs Parian wreaths;
A swan-like form invests the hidden thorn;
Fills up the farmer's lane from wall to wall,

Maugre the farmer's sighs; and, at the gate,
A tapering turret overtops the work.
And when his hours are numbered, and the world
Is all his own, retiring, as he were not,
Leaves, when the sun appears, astonished Art
To mimic in slow structures, stone by stone,
Built in an age, the mad wind's night-work,
The frolic architecture of the snow.

LOW BAROMETER
ROBERT BRIDGES

The south-wind strengthens to a gale,
Across the moon the clouds fly fast,
The house is smitten as with a flail,
The chimney shudders to the blast.

On such a night, when Air has loosed
Its guardian grasp on blood and brain,
Old terrors then of god or ghost
Creep from their caves to life again;

And Reason kens he herits in
A haunted house. Tenants unknown
Assert their squalid lease of sin
With earlier title than his own.

Unbodied presences, the pack'd
Pollution and remorse of Time,
Slipp'd from oblivion reënact
The horrors of unhouseld crime.

Some men would quell the thing with prayer

Whose sightless footsteps pad the floor,
Whose fearful trespass mounts the stair
Or burts the lock'd forbidden door.

Some have seen corpses long interr'd
Escape from hallowing control,
Pale charnel forms—nay ev'n have heard
The shrilling of a troubled soul,

That wanders till the dawn hath cross'd
The dolorous dark, or Earth hath wound
Closer her storm-spredd cloke, and thrust
The baleful phantoms underground.

A LINE-STORM SONG

ROBERT FROST

The line-storm clouds fly tattered and swift,
  The road is forlorn all day,
Where a myriad snowy quartz stones lift,
  And the hoof-prints vanish away.
The roadside flowers, too wet for the bee,
  Expend their bloom in vain.
Come over the hills and far with me,
  And be my love in the rain.

The birds have less to say for themselves
  In the wood-world's torn despair
Than now these numberless years the elves,
  Although they are no less there:
All song of the woods is crushed like some
  Wild, easily shattered rose.
Come, be my love in the wet woods; come,
  Where the boughs rain when it blows.

There is the gale to urge behind
  And bruit our singing down,
And the shallow waters aflutter with wind

From which to gather your gown.
What matter if we go clear to the west,
  And come not through dry-shod?
For wilding brooch shall wet your breast
  The rain-fresh goldenrod.

Oh, never this whelming east wind swells
  But it seems like the sea's return
To the ancient lands where it left the shells
  Before the age of the fern;
And it seems like the time when after doubt
  Our love came back amain.
Oh, come forth into the storm and rout
  And be my love in the rain.

A MOUNTAIN STORM

KATHERINE LEE BATES

Our blue sierras shone serene, sublime,
When ghostly shapes came crowding up the air,
Shadowing the landscape with some vast despair;
And all was changed as in weird pantomime,
Transfigured into vague, fantastic form
By that tremendous carnival of storm.
Pilgrim processions of bowed trees that climb
To sacred summits, in the clashing hail
Shuddered like flagellants beneath the flail.
Most gracious hills, in that tempestuous time,
Went wild as angered bulls, with bellowing cry
And goring horns that strove to charge the sky.
Masses of rock, long gnawed by stealthy rime,
With sudden roar that made our bravest blanch,
Came volleying down in fatal avalanche.
All nature seemed convulsed in some fierce crime,
And then a rainbow, and behold! the sun
Went comforting the harebells one by one;
And all was still save for the vesper chime
From far, faint belfry bathed in creamy light,
And the soft footfalls of the coming night.

SPRING

ABOUT HANS CHRISTIAN ANDERSEN

Hans Christian Andersen was born in 1805 in Denmark. As a child, he went to school and worked for a weaver and tailor, respectively. When he was 14, he went to Copenhagen in hopes that he could become an actor. He worked with the Royal Danish Theatre as a singer until his voice changed. King Frederick VI paid for Andersen's grammar schooling at the prompting of the director of the Royal Danish Theatre. Andersen's school years were a struggle, because his teachers didn't support him in his writing, and his schoolmaster physically abused him. He died in 1875.

Andersen is primarily known today for his fairy tales, but he also wrote plays, travelogues, novels, and poems. His early fairy tales were retellings of the stories he heard as a child. He went on to write around 3,381 fairy tales in his life. In 1829, he wrote a strange short story called "A Journey on Foot from Holmen's Canal to the East Point of Amager," which gained a decent amount of popularity. When his fairy tales were able to be translated in 1845, he gained more popularity. "The Little Mermaid" was one of these translated tales.

THE STORM SHAKES THE SHIELD
HANS CHRISTIAN ANDERSEN

In the old days, when grandpapa was quite a little boy, and ran about in little red breeches and a red coat, and a feather in his cap—for that's the costume the little boys wore in his time when they were dressed in their best—many things were very different from what they are now. There was often a good deal of show in the streets—show that we don't see nowadays, because it has been abolished as too old-fashioned. Still, it is very interesting to hear grandfather tell about it.

It must really have been a gorgeous sight to behold, in those days, when the shoemaker brought over the shield, when the court-house was changed. The silken flag waved to and fro, on the shield itself a double eagle was displayed, and a big boot; the youngest lads carried the "welcome," and the chest of the workmen's guild, and their shirt-sleeves were adorned with red and white ribbons; the elder ones carried drawn swords, each with a lemon stuck on its point. There was a full band of music, and the most splendid of all the instruments was the "bird," as grandfather called the big stick with the crescent on the top, and all manner of dingle-dangles hanging to it—a perfect

Turkish clatter of music. The stick was lifted high in the air, and swung up and down till it jingled again, and quite dazzled one's eyes when the sun shone on all its glory of gold, and silver, and brass.

In front of the procession ran the Harlequin, dressed in clothes made of all kinds of colored patches artfully sewn together, with a black face, and bells on his head like a sledge horse. He beat the people with his bat, which made a great clattering without hurting them, and the people would crowd together and fall back, only to advance again the next moment. Little boys and girls fell over their own toes into the gutter, old women dispensed digs with their elbows, and looked sour, and took snuff. One laughed, another chatted; the people thronged the windows and door-steps, and even all the roofs. The sun shone; and although they had a little rain too, that was good for the farmer; and when they got wetted thoroughly, they only thought what a blessing it was for the country.

And what stories grandpapa could tell! As a little boy he had seen all these fine doings in their greatest pomp. The oldest of the policemen used to make a speech from the platform on which the shield was hung up, and the speech was in verse, as if it had been made by a poet, as, indeed it had; for three people had concocted it together, and they had first drunk a good bowl of punch, so that the speech might turn out well.

And the people gave a cheer for the speech, but they shouted much louder for the Harlequin, when he appeared in front of the platform, and made a grimace at them.

The fools played the fool most admirably, and drank mead out of spirit-glasses, which they then flung among the crowd, by whom they were caught up. Grandfather was the possessor of one of these glasses, which had been given him by a working mason, who had managed to catch it. Such a scene was really very pleasant; and the shield on the new court-house was hung with flowers and green wreaths.

"One never forgets a feast like that, however old one may grow," said grandfather. Nor did he forget it, though he saw many other grand spectacles in his time, and could tell about them too; but it was most pleasant of all to hear him tell about the shield that was brought in the town from the old to the new court-house.

Once, when he was a little boy, grandpapa had gone with his parents to see this festivity. He had never yet been in the metropolis of the country. There were so many people in the streets, that he thought that the shield was being carried. There were many shields to be seen; a hundred rooms might have been filled with pictures, if they had been hung up inside and outside. At the tailor's were pictures of all kinds of clothing, to show that he could stitch up people from the coarsest to the finest; at the tobacco manufacturer's were pictures of the most charming little boys, smoking cigars, just as they do in reality; there were signs with painted butter, and herring, clerical collars, and coffins, and inscriptions and announcements into the bargain. A person could walk up and down for a whole day through the streets, and tire himself out with looking at the pictures; and then he would know all about what people lived in the houses, for they had hung out their shields or signs; and, as grandfather said, it was a very instructive thing, in a great town, to know at once who the inhabitants were.

And this is what happened with these shields, when

grandpapa came to the town. He told it me himself, and he hadn't "a rogue on his back," as mother used to tell me he had when he wanted to make me believe something outrageous, for now he looked quite trustworthy.

The first night after he came to the town had been signalized by the most terrible gale ever recorded in the newspapers—a gale such as none of the inhabitants had ever before experienced. The air was dark with flying tiles; old wood-work crashed and fell; and a wheelbarrow ran up the streets all alone, only to get out of the way. There was a groaning in the air, and a howling and a shrieking, and altogether it was a terrible storm. The water in the canal rose over the banks, for it did not know where to run. The storm swept over the town, carrying plenty of chimneys with it, and more than one proud weathercock on a church tower had to bow, and has never got over it from that time.

There was a kind of sentry-house, where dwelt the venerable old superintendent of the fire brigade, who always arrived with the last engine. The storm would not leave this little sentry-house alone, but must needs tear it from its fastenings, and roll it down the street; and, wonderfully enough, it stopped opposite to the door of the dirty journeyman plasterer, who had saved three lives at the last fire, but the sentry-house thought nothing of that.

The barber's shield, the great brazen dish, was carried away, and hurled straight into the embrasure of the councillor of justice; and the whole neighborhood said this looked almost like malice, inasmuch as they, and nearly all the friends of the councillor's wife, used to call that lady "the Razor" for she was so sharp that she knew more about other people's business than they knew about it themselves.

A shield with a dried salt fish painted on it flew exactly

in front of the door of a house where dwelt a man who wrote a newspaper. That was a very poor joke perpetrated by the gale, which seemed to have forgotten that a man who writes in a paper is not the kind of person to understand any liberty taken with him; for he is a king in his own newspaper, and likewise in his own opinion.

The weathercock flew to the opposite house, where he perched, looking the picture of malice—so the neighbors said.

The cooper's tub stuck itself up under the head of "ladies' costumes."

The eating-house keeper's bill of fare, which had hung at his door in a heavy frame, was posted by the storm over the entrance to the theatre, where nobody went. "It was a ridiculous list—horse-radish, soup, and stuffed cabbage." And now people came in plenty.

The fox's skin, the honorable sign of the furrier, was found fastened to the bell-pull of a young man who always went to early lecture, and looked like a furled umbrella. He said he was striving after truth, and was considered by his aunt "a model and an example."

The inscription "Institution for Superior Education" was found near the billiard club, which place of resort was further adorned with the words, "Children brought up by hand." Now, this was not at all witty; but, you see, the storm had done it, and no one has any control over that.

It was a terrible night, and in the morning—only think!—nearly all the shields had changed places. In some places the inscriptions were so malicious, that grandfather would not speak of them at all; but I saw that he was chuckling secretly, and there may have been some inaccuracy in his description, after all.

The poor people in the town, and still more the strangers, were continually making mistakes in the people they wanted to see; nor was this to be avoided, when they went according to the shields that were hung up. Thus, for instance, some who wanted to go to a very grave assembly of elderly men, where important affairs were to be discussed, found themselves in a noisy boys' school, where all the company were leaping over the chairs and tables.

There were also people who made a mistake between the church and the theatre, and that was terrible indeed!

Such a storm we have never witnessed in our day; for that only happened in grandpapa's time, when he was quite a little boy. Perhaps we shall never experience a storm of the kind, but our grandchildren may; and we can only hope and pray that all may stay at home while the storm is moving the shields.

EMILY DICKINSON

Emily Elizabeth Dickinson was an American poet from Amherst, Massachusetts. She was born December 10, 1830 into a middle-class family with an older brother, William Austin, and a younger sister, Lavinia Norcross. Emily's father strived for her and her siblings to have an education. Emily later studied at Amherst Academy where she learned subjects like Latin, Botany, and Mental Philosophy. Emily was known to have a very introverted personality. It was believed that she may have suffered from mental illness, or anxiety disorders. Emily's mother became ill in the mid 1850s which began Emily's life of isolation, living among nature and books. She wrote until her death in 1886, although she ceased organizing and editing.

A vast majority of her poems were published after her death, though there were few published during her life. Dickinson was popular for her uniquely written poems which include short line, a lack of titles, and irregular use of capitalization and punctuation. Emily enjoyed contemporary popular literature and was likely influenced by Henry Wadsworth Longfellow, Charlotte Brontë, and William Shakespeare. During her mother's illness, Emily wrote her more famous works, though she had written many poems in her early years. Between 1858 and 1865, Emily wrote about forty different collections filled with her poems, totaling to almost eight hundred poems all together.

A THUNDER-STORM

EMILY DICKINSON

The wind begun to rock the grass
With threatening tunes and low, —
He flung a menace at the earth,
A menace at the sky.

The leaves unhooked themselves from trees
And started all abroad;
The dust did scoop itself like hands
And throw away the road.

The wagons quickened on the streets,
The thunder hurried slow;
The lightning showed a yellow beak,
And then a livid claw.

The birds put up the bars to nests,
The cattle fled to barns;
There came one drop of giant rain,
And then, as if the hands

That held the dams had parted hold,

The waters wrecked the sky,
But overlooked my father's house,
Just quartering a tree.

A CONTRAST
THOMAS DURFEE

Once, in an old and lonely
Farm-house by the sea,
I went to rest with only
Myself for company.

No star the darkness brightened;
Alow the welkin bowed;
It blew, it rained, it lightened,
It thundered long and loud.

The tempest drove the billows
Upon the rocky shore,
And, nestled in my pillows,
I heard them plunge and roar.

The windows creaked and rattled,
The chimney puffed and moaned,
The stout old elms, that battled
Out in the court-yard, groaned.

I dozed while yet I listened;

And lo! the next I knew,
The golden sunshine glistened,
And everything was new.

The cock was crowing clearly,
Cluck-clucked the happy hen,
The robin carolled cheerly,
And sweetly chirped the wren.

I rose with glad emotion
And up the window threw;
Before me heaved the ocean
Its sparkling waters blue.

The skies were soft and tender;
And lovely to be seen.
Impearled with dewy splendor,
The land lay fresh and green.

I breathed an air Elysian;
I thrilled with pure delight;
And nothing but a vision
Seemed that black yester-night.

EDGAR ALLAN POE

Edgar Allan Poe was born in 1809 in Boston Massachusetts to two actors. His mother died in 1811, a year after his father left her. This left Poe as an orphan, but the merchant John Allan took him under his care. Poe went on to join the army to make a living, but later purposely got himself court-martialed. In 1835, he obtained a license to marry his 13-year-old cousin, Virginia Clemm. A man named Joseph W. Walker found him in a delirious state, wearing someone else's clothing. He died in the hospital that day. Even today, his cause of death is unknown.

Poe is known as the pioneer in detective fiction and as a contributor to the genre of science fiction. His writings remain popular even today and have a reputation of being macabre. He was the first writer in the United States to try to make a career out of writing, but he faced financial troubles throughout his life. After the publication of his poem, "The Raven," in 1845, Poe became famous. He wrote Gothic pieces, because the public enjoyed the dark genre at the time. Poe found more popularity in Europe than the United States though. Most people knew Poe more for his critique work, not his writing.

ALONE

EDGAR ALLAN POE

From childhood's hour I have not been
As others were—I have not seen
As others saw—I could not bring
My passions from a common spring—
From the same source I have not taken
My sorrow—I could not awaken
My heart to joy at the same tone—
And all I lov'd—I lov'd alone—
Then—in my childhood—in the dawn
Of a most stormy life—was drawn
From ev'ry depth of good and ill
The mystery which binds me still—
From the torrent, or the fountain—
From the red cliff of the mountain—
From the sun that 'round me roll'd
In its autumn tint of gold—
From the lightning in the sky
As it pass'd me flying by—
From the thunder, and the storm—
And the cloud that took the form
(When the rest of Heaven was blue)
Of a demon in my view—

HENRY WADSWORTH LONGFELLOW

Henry Wadsworth Longfellow was born February 27, 1807, in Portland, Maine (then a part of Massachusetts). He began schooling at age three with his older brother in private schooling, preparing for a later entrance into Bowdoin College. Longfellow passed the entrance exam at age 13, but his parents chose to delay the move to Brunswick for another year and had him study at Portland Academy as a freshman. Although his father preferred him for a career in law, Longfellow directed his studies toward literature. Longfellow spent three years traveling Europe to prepare for a professorship at Bowdoin by developing linguistic fluency. After returning from Europe he married Mary Potter in 1831. The couple miscarried in October 1935 and Mary died in November due to health issues. Longfellow spent more time in Europe and returned to poetry, falling in love with Frances Appleton and later marrying her in 1843. They had six children. Longfellow died from phlebitis less than a month after his 75th birthday.

Longfellow writing displays a variety of poetic styles in both fictional and nonfictional prose. He was first published at the age of 13 in the Portland Gazette. Some of his best known works include "Paul Revere's Ride," Evangeline, A Tale of Acadie, and "A Psalm of Life". "The Rainy Day", a poem featured in this anthology, was published in 1842 as part of the collection Ballads and Other Poems where Longfellow was exploring American subject matter and dramatic writing.

THE RAINY DAY
HENRY WADSWORTH LONGFELLOW

The day is cold, and dark, and dreary;
It rains, and the wind is never weary;
The vine still clings to the mouldering wall,
But at every gust the dead leaves fall,
And the day is dark and dreary.

My life is cold, and dark, and dreary;
It rains,and the wind is never weary;
My thoughts still cling to the mouldering past,
But the hopes of youth fall thick in the blast,
And the days are dark and dreary.

Be still, sad heart, and cease repining;
Behind the clouds is the sun still shining;
Thy fate is the common fate of all,
Into each life some rain must fall,
Some days must be dark and dreary.

THE RISING OF THE STORM

PAUL LAURENCE DUNBAR

The lake's dark breast
Is all unrest,
It heaves with a sob and a sigh.
Like a tremulous bird,
From its slumber stirred,
The moon is a–tilt in the sky.

From the silent deep
The waters sweep,
But faint on the cold white stones,
And the wavelets fly
With a plaintive cry
O'er the old earth's bare, bleak bones.

And the spray upsprings
On its ghost–white wings,
And tosses a kiss at the stars;
While a water–sprite,
In sea–pearls dight,
Hums a sea–hymn's solemn bars.

Far out in the night,

On the wavering sight
I see a dark hull loom;
And its light on high,
Like a Cyclops' eye,
Shines out through the mist and gloom.

Now the winds well up
From the earth's deep cup,
And fall on the sea and shore,
And against the pier
The waters rear
And break with a sullen roar.

Up comes the gale,
And the mist–wrought veil
Gives way to the lightning's glare,
And the cloud–drifts fall,
A sombre pall,
O'er water, earth, and air.

The storm–king flies,
His whip he plies,
And bellows down the wind.
The lightning rash
With blinding flash
Comes pricking on behind.

Rise, waters, rise,
And taunt the skies
With your swift–flitting form.
Sweep, wild winds, sweep,
And tear the deep

To atoms in the storm.

And the waters leapt,
And the wild winds swept,
And blew out the moon in the sky,
And I laughed with glee,
It was joy to me
As the storm went raging by!

SQUALL

LEONORA SPEYER

The squall sweeps gray-winged across the obliterated
hills,
    And the startled lake seems to run before it;
    From the wood comes a clamor of leaves,
    Tugging at the twigs,
    Pouring from the branches,
    And suddenly the birds are still.

    Thunder crumples the sky,
    Lightning tears at it.

    And now the rain!
    The rain—thudding—implacable—
    The wind, reveling in the confusion of great pines!

    And a silver sifting of light,
    A coolness;
    A sense of summer anger passing,
    Of summer gentleness creeping nearer—
    Penitent, tearful,
    Forgiven!

STORM ENDING

JEAN TOOMER

Thunder blossoms gorgeously above our heads,
Great, hollow, bell-like flowers,
Rumbling in the wind,
Stretching clappers to strike our ears . . .
Full-lipped flowers
Bitten by the sun
Bleeding rain
Dripping rain like golden honey—
And the sweet earth flying from the thunder.

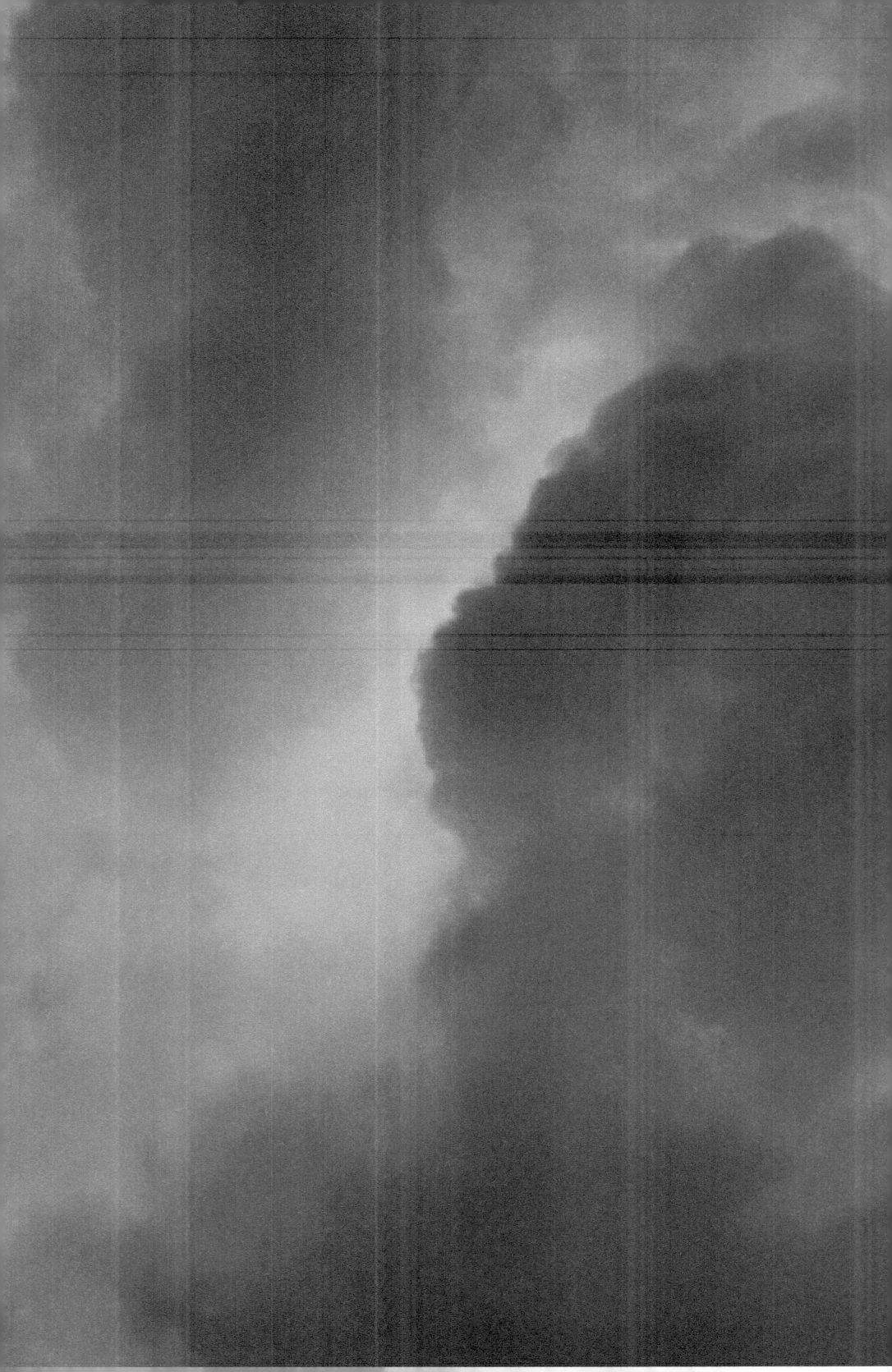

SUMMER

SUMMER SNOW STORM

ADAM CHASE

*Snow in summer is of course impossible. Any weather expert will
tell you so. Weather Bureau Chief Botts was certain no such
absurdity could occur. And he would have been right except for one
thing. It snowed that summer.*

It was as the expression goes, raining cats and dogs.
Since the Weather Bureau had predicted fair and warmer,
the Weather Bureau was not particularly happy about
the meteorological state of affairs. No one, however was
shocked.

Until it started to snow.

This was on the twenty-fifth of July in the U.S.A....

Half an hour before the fantastic meteorological turn
of events, Bureau Chief Botts dangled the forecast sheet
before Johnny Sloman's bloodshot eyes and barked, "It's
all over the country by now, you dunderhead!" Then, as an
afterthought: "Did you write this?"

"Yes," said Sloman miserably.

Slowly, Botts said, "Temperature, eighty degrees.
Precipitation expected: snow. Snow, Sloman. Well, that's
what it says."

"It was a mistake, Chief. Just—heh-heh—a mistake."

"The prediction should have been for fair and warmer!" Botts screamed.

"But it's raining," Sloman pointed out.

"We make mistakes," said Botts in a suddenly velvety voice. Then, as if that had been a mistake, bellowed: "But not this kind of mistake, Sloman! Snow in July! We have a reputation to maintain! If not for accuracy, at least for credulity."

"Yes, sir," said Johnny Sloman. One of the troubles was, he had a hangover. Although, actually, that was a consequence of the real trouble. The real trouble was his fiancee. Make that his ex-fiancee. Because last night Jo-Anne had left him. "You—you're just going no place at all, Johnny Sloman," she had said. "You're on a treadmill and—not even running very fast." She had given him back the quarter-carat ring tearfully, but Johnny hadn't argued. Jo-Anne had a stubborn streak and he knew when Jo-Anne's mind was made up. So Johnny had gone and gotten drunk for the first time since the night after college graduation, not too many years ago, and the result was a nationally-distributed forecast of snow.

Chief Botts' first flush of anger had now been replaced by self-pity. His red, loose-jowled face was sagging and his eyes became watery as he said, "At least you could have double-checked it. As a member of this Bureau you only have to fill out the forecast once every ten days. Is that so hard? Is there any reason why you should predict snow for July 25th?" His voice became silky soft as he added, "You realize, of course, Sloman, that if this was anything but a civil service job you'd be out on your ear for a stunt like this! Well, there are other ways. I can pass over you for promotion. I intend to pass over you until the crack of doom. You'll be a GS-5 the rest of your working life. Are you satisfied, Sloman? Snow in July ..." Chief Botts' voice trailed off, the Chief following it.

Johnny sat with his head in his hands until Harry Bettis, the GS-5 weatherman who shared his small office with him, came in. Naturally, hangover or no, Johnny had reported for work first. Johnny was always first in the office, but it didn't seem to do any good. Now, Harry Bettis could come in an hour late and read the funnies half the day and flirt with the secretarial staff the other half and still be Chief Botts' odds-on favorite for the promotion that was opening next month. Harry Bettis was like that.

He came in and gave Johnny the full treatment. First the slow spreading smile. Then the chuckle. Then the loud, roaring belly-laugh. "Gals outside told me!" he shouted, loud enough so the girls outside would know he knew they had told him. "Snow! Snow in July! Sloman, you kill me! You really do!"

"Do you have to shout?" Johnny said.

"Do I? We all ought to shout this. To the rooftops! Sloman, my foot. You have a new name, sonny. Snowman! Johnny Snowman."

Johnny groaned. Instinctively, he knew the name would stick.

"Hear you had a little trouble with the gal-friend this past p.m.," Harry Bettis clucked in a voice which managed to be both derisive and sympathetic.

"How did you find out?" Johnny asked, but knew the answer at once. Jo-Anne was a roommate of one of the Bureau Secretaries. It was how Johnny had met her.

"You know how I found out, Snowman. Well, that's

tough luck, kiddo. But tell me, does that mean the field is wide open? I always thought your gal-friend—your ex-gal-friend—had the cutest pair of—"

"I have nothing to do with whether the field is open or not open, I'm afraid."

"Well, don't be. Afraid, I mean," Harry Bettis advised jovially. "If the gal could make you pull a boner like that, you're better off without her. But I forgot to ask Maxine: can I have little Jo-Anne's phone number? Huh, boy?"

Before Johnny could answer, the three-girl staff of secretaries entered the small office. Entered—and stared.

"That's all right, girls," Harry Bettis said. "You didn't have to follow me in here. I'd have been right out."

But they weren't staring at Harry Bettis. They were staring at Johnny. Their mouths had flapped open, their eyes were big and round. Johnny didn't, but Harry Bettis knew that look on a girl's face. Without any trouble at all, Johnny could have made any of those girls, right there, right then, without even trying.

They gawked and gawked. One of them pointed at the window. The others tried to, but their hands were trembling.

The one who was pointing squawked: "Look!"

The second one said, "Out the window!"

The third one said, "Will you!"

Outside the window on the twenty-fifth of July it was snowing.

It was an hour later. Telephones were ringing. Long-distance calls from all over the country now that the ticker had gone out with the incredible fact that it was snowing in the Northeast in July. Most of the calls, though, were from Washington. Chief Botts disconnected the PBX and walked in a dazed, staggering fashion to Johnny, smiling weakly and saying:

"Sloman, I misjudged you. Genius, right here, right now, in this office, and we never knew it. Sloman, I have to admit I was wrong about you. But how did you know? How did you ever know?"

"Hell's bells," Harry Bettis said before Johnny could say it was all a mistake. "That's easy, Chief. Anyone knows that all rain starts out as snow. It's got to. You see, the droplets of moisture in the cold upper regions of a cloud condense around dust particles because the air up there is too cold to hold them as vapor. Since it's below freezing, snow is formed—snow which warms up as it passes through hotter air en route to the ground, and—"

"That will be quite enough, Bettis," Chief Botts said. "I am a weatherman too, you know. You don't have to tell me the most elementary of—"

"In this case, Chief," Bettis persisted, "the biggest inversion layer you ever saw kept the surface air down and brought the cold upper air very close to the surface. Result: the snowflakes didn't have a chance to melt, not even to freezing rain. Result: snow!"

"The chances of that happening," said Chief Botts coldly, "are about one in a billion. Aren't they, Sloman, dear fellow?"

"One in two billion," Johnny said.

"He is modest," Chief Botts told the staff. "He seems so unconcerned."

Just then Maxine came into the little office. The look of awe on her face had been replaced by one of sheer amazement. "Well, I checked it, Chief," she said. "Wait until I tell Jo-Anne!"

"Won't you please tell us first?" Chief Botts asked.

"Yes, sir," said Maxine, and read from the memo pad in her hand. "Since coming to work for the Bureau, Johnny Sloman has once every ten days made our official forecast. I have checked back on his forecast, Chief, as you directed. Johnny has made fifty-five forecasts. While only one of them—startlingly—has called for snow in July—every single one of them has been right."

There was a shocked silence. "But—but the Weather Bureau average is only eighty-eight percent!" Harry Bettis gasped.

"You mean," Chief Botts corrected him, "eighty-eight percent is the figure we try to foist on the unsuspecting public. Actually, the Weather Bureau averages a bare seventy-five percent, and you know it."

"But Sloman's got a hundred percent accuracy—up to and including snow in July," Harry Bettis said in a shocked voice.

"It was only an accident," Johnny said in a mild voice. "I didn't mean to write snow."

"Accident, smaccident," said Harry Bettis. "It was no accident with a record like that. You have the uncanny ability to forecast weather with complete accuracy, Johnny-boy. You realize what that means, old pal?"

"I'd better call Washington and tell them," Chief Botts said, but Harry Bettis held his arm while Johnny mused:

"I guess I realize what it means, Harry. That is, if you're right. No more getting wet on picnics. Because I'd know. I'd know, Harry. No more going to ball games and having them rained out on you. No more being caught by a thunderstorm at the beach ..."

"Johnny!" Harry Bettis said. "Think, pal. Think!"

"I'm calling Washington," Chief Botts said. "This is too much for me."

But Harry Bettis was still holding his arm. "Now, just a minute, bucko," he said. "You're not calling anyone—not without his manager's permission."

"Whose manager's permission?"

"Why, Mr. Sloman's manager's permission, of course. In a word, me."

"This is preposterous!" Chief Botts cried.

"Is it?" Bettis asked. "Listen, Johnny, don't let anyone sell you a bill of goods—like the Civil Service Commission giving you a GS-8 rating and sending you to Washington. Because stick with me, kid, and there'll be great things in store for you, you'll see."

"Such," said Maxine dubiously, "as what?"

"Are you on our side?" Harry Bettis asked her suspiciously.

"I'm on Jo-Anne's side. If old Johnny here has something she ought to have, I want to know it."

"You mean, if she ought to change her mind and marry him? I'll admit it even if I think Jo-Anne's a real cute trick: she'd be nuts if she didn't." Women, Harry Bettis did not add, never came between Harry Bettis and ten percent of a gold mine. But that's what he was thinking. He went on: "Just think of it, Johnny. Drought in the Midwest. They call Sloman. Sloman predicts rain. It rains. Have any idea what they'd pay for a stunt like that? Or swollen rivers in New England, or California. Looks like another big flood is on the way, but they call Sloman. Looks like rain, kiddo? That don't matter. Predict a dry spell and it won't rain. Do you know," Harry Bettis said in a devout whisper, "what a stunt like that would be worth? Millions."

"Yeah, wise guy," said Maxine. "So what's in it for you?"

Harry Bettis did not look at Maxine when he answered. He looked at Johnny and said, "I'll be frank, kiddo. You have the talent, but you don't have the salesmanship to promote it. Do you want a mediocre job while the weather boys exploit you for the rest of your life or—do you want greatness, riches, and Jo-Anne?"

"Jo-Anne," Johnny said.

Harry Bettis nodded. "My price is twenty-five percent."

"Of Jo-Anne?" Maxine asked suspiciously.

"Of everything Johnny makes as the world's first real Weather Man. Not a forecaster—a commander. Because when my client forecasts the weather, it happens. Brothers and sisters, it happens." He turned abruptly to Johnny, said, "You have any money saved up?"

"A few hundred dollars, but—"

"An ad in the papers. Alongside the article telling how it snowed on July twenty-fifth. Saying that your services are for hire. We're a shoo-in, kid!"

"Well, if you say so," Johnny said doubtfully.

"So don't call D.C.," Bettis told Chief Botts.

"But Sloman's an employee of this Bureau."

"Was, you mean."

"What did you say?"

"Was an employee. He ain't an employee now. He's quitting—with his manager," said Harry Bettis, and walked out of the office, steering a dazed Johnny Sloman with him.

"Wait until I call Jo-Anne," Maxine said.

During the next six months, Johnny Sloman—known to the world as The Weather Man—made fifty million dollars. Since it had taken a whole lifetime for him to

develop his remarkable talent, his lawyers were trying to
have capital gains declared on the earnings rather than
straight income tax. The odds seemed to be in their favor.

How had Johnny made his fifty million dollars? By
predicting the weather. He predicted:

A flood in the Texas panhandle—in time to save the
dry lands from going entirely arid.

An end of the snowstorms in northern Canada—which
had trapped the five hundred residents of a small uranium-
mining town without food or adequate drinking water.

The break-up of Hurricane Anita—which had
threatened to be the most destructive ever to strike the
Carolina Coast.

No frost for Florida that winter—a prediction still to
be ascertained, but a foregone conclusion.

Every prediction had come true. In time, the world
began to realize that his predictions were not predictions
at all: they were sure things. That is, they predicted
nothing—they made things happen. Johnny was in demand
everywhere and naturally could not fill all engagements.
Harry Bettis hired a whole squad of corresponding
secretaries, whose job it was to turn down, with regret,
some ninety percent of the jobs requested. Johnny, in fact,
was in such demand, that his engagement to Jo-Anne—
which, of course, had been reinstated at her insistence—
remained only an engagement. The nuptials were put off,
and put off again.

This suited Harry Bettis, who saw to it that Johnny
kept putting off the marriage. Because, ultimately, Jo-Anne
would reach the end of her proverbial tether and decide
that Harry's twenty-five percent, if it could be shared as
a wife, was better than Johnny's seventy-five percent, if it

could not.

Jo-Anne, though, was not that kind of girl. Harry Bettis, knowing no other kind of girl, never understood that.

The scientists, meanwhile, had a field day with Johnny. His strange talent obeyed no natural law, they said, and at first attributed it to random chance. Soon, though, this became patently impossible. And so a new natural law was sought. All types of hair-brained theories were proposed, none of them accepted, until an osteopathic physician in Duluth, Minn., hit upon the theory that staggered the world with its simplicity and, eventually, was accepted as that which explained the strange phenomenon of Johnny Sloman.

The osteopath, many of whose patients suffered from rheumatism which was aggravated by the bitter Minnesota winters, suggested that Johnny Sloman was a case of rheumatism in reverse. The weather, he pointed out, had an adverse effect upon the symptoms of his patients. Conversely, why couldn't some human being—a Johnny Sloman, for example—affect the weather in precisely the same way that the weather invariably affected his rheumatic patients?

It was clear, simple, lucid. It was the only theory which could not be disproven by the weight of scientific knowledge. It thus became the accepted theory.

"The Under-Secretary of Defense to see you," Maxine said one day during the winter following Johnny's July snowfall.

"Don't see him," Harry Bettis said. "You don't want to see him."

"But why not?" Johnny asked.

"Because they'll make you a dollar-a-year man and we're not in this to make any stinking dollar a year," Harry Bettis said.

"Well, I think I ought to see him, anyway. At least see him." He turned to Jo-Anne, who was sitting at the next desk, writing up some reports. "What do you think, Jo?"

"If the country needs you, Johnny," she said, "it's your duty to help."

Johnny told Maxine, "Show the Under-Secretary in, please."

He was a small man with a big brief case. He spoke slowly, earnestly, backing up his statements with reams of paper from the brief case. The Defense Department had not contacted Johnny right away, he said, because they wanted to compile all the facts. They had all the facts now.

Johnny Sloman could be the biggest single factor for peace the world had ever known.

Item. In the event of aggression, he could so bog down the aggressor's supply lines and troop movements with continuous rains and snowstorms that it would be all but impossible for the aggressor to maintain hostilities.

Item. In the event that such tactical weather-war failed, he could cause a drought in the aggressor's food-producing regions, forcing the aggressor to surrender or face starvation.

Item. He could always, conversely, see to it that the defensive force's supply lines were never hampered by the weather and that the precipitation over the defensive country's breadbasket was ideal.

Item. He could render aggressor communication difficult with heavy fog and/or icy roads.

Item. He could cover defensive troop movements with

low, dense clouds.

In short, concluded the Under-Secretary, Johnny Sloman could be a one-man world police-force practically guaranteeing peace. He stopped talking. He looked at Johnny. His eyes said, the call of duty is clear.

Harry Bettis said, "Well, thank you for your time, Mr. Secretary. Naturally, we'll think about what you said."

"Think about it!" gasped the Under-Secretary. "Think about it!"

"My client is a busy man—the busiest man in his field," Harry Bettis said.

The Under-Secretary smiled bleakly. "The only man in his field, you mean. That's why we need him."

"We'll send you a report in a few weeks," Harry said indifferently, "after we've had an opportunity to study the situation."

"But, Harry—" Johnny began.

"Johnny," Harry said. He did not have to finish the statement. It had happened before—"Johnny, I've made you a tremendous success. I'm your manager, aren't I? Let's leave it that way."

"If Johnny thinks he ought to help—" Jo-Anne said.

"Now, Jo-Anne," Harry Bettis scolded, and led the Under-Secretary to the door.

Three days later, the assistant chief of the F.B.I. came to see them. "We regret this, Sloman," he said.

"You regret what?" Harry Bettis asked.

"Defense allowed a report on its findings out. That was unwise. We'll have to give you around-the-clock protection, Sloman."

"Protection from what?" Johnny wanted to know.

"Enemy agents. The enemy is desperate. At all costs, according to their intelligence reports, they're out to get you."

"Get him?" said Harry Bettis. "You mean, kill him?"

"I mean, get him. Get him on their side. Because everything Johnny could do for the forces of peace and democracy, he could be made to do for the forces of aggression. You see?"

"Yes," said Johnny.

"No," said Harry Bettis. "This sounds like a government trick—to make Johnny go to work. To make him think it's his patriotic duty—"

"Well," said Jo-Anne sharply, "isn't it?"

Harry Bettis smiled. "When he gets as big as Universal Motors, he can become patriotic."

"Mr. Sloman," the assistant F.B.I. chief said, "they will either try to kidnap you outright, or work on you through someone you love. Therefore, our bodyguards—"

"Well, let them keep their distance, that's all," Bettis said. "Bad for business. Nobody wants enemy agents hanging around."

"That's your final decision?" the F.B.I. man asked.

"Well—" began Johnny.

"Yes, it's our final decision," said Harry Bettis, showing the F.B.I. man to the door.

"I don't think you should have done that," Johnny said after he had gone.

"You just make the weather, Johnny-boy. I'll take care of business."

"Well—" said Johnny.

"Johnny!" cried Jo-Anne. "Oh, Johnny! Why don't you act like a man?" And she ran from the room, slamming the door.

After that, Johnny didn't see her again.

She was gone.

Really gone, for certain, not simply walking off in a huff.

Two weeks later, Johnny got the letter—unofficial—from the Enemy.

The F.B.I. was sympathetic, but the Chief said, "You can understand, Mr. Sloman, how our hands are tied. It is not an official letter. We can't prove anything. We don't doubt it for a minute, of course. The cold war enemy has kidnapped your fiancee and taken her to their motherland. But—we can't prove it. Not being able to prove it, we can't do a thing about it. You're aware, of course, of how readily the rest of the world condemns our actions. Not that they wouldn't be on our side if we could prove that this kidnap letter was the real thing, but you realize we won't be able to prove it at all."

"Oh," said Johnny. He went home. He saw Harry Bettis, who said he was shocked. The note read:

Mr. Johnny Sloman:

We have Miss Jo-Anne Davis here in the motherland. The only way she can live a normal life here is if you join her and work for us. We believe you know what the other kind of life is like here.

Bettis said, "It stumps the hell out of me, Johnny."

"I'm just waking up," said Johnny slowly. "In a way, it's your fault."

"Now, don't be a jackass, Johnny."

Jackass or no, Johnny hit him. His knuckles went crunch and Harry Bettis' nose went crunch and Bettis fell down. He lay there, his nose not looking so good.

Now, when it was apparently too late, Johnny knew what his course of action should have been. Get rid of the money-grubbing Bettis. Go to work for the government unselfishly. Insure world peace.

Too late ... too late ...

Because unless he could somehow save Jo-Anne, he would never predict the weather again—for anyone.

"But what you ask is impossible!" the Secretary of Defense said a few days later.

"If I come back, if I'm successful," Johnny said quietly, "I'm your man, for as long as you want me, without pay."

"You mean that?" the Secretary asked slowly.

"I mean it."

The Secretary nodded grimly, touched a button on his desk. "Get me Air Force Chief of Staff Burns," he said, and, a moment later: "Bernie? Chuck here. We need a plane. A jet-transport to go you-know-where. Cargo? One man, in a parachute. Can you manage it? Immediately, if not sooner. Good boy, Bernie. No ... no, I'm sorry, I can't tell you a thing about it." The Secretary cut the connection, turned to Johnny:

"You leave this afternoon, Sloman. You realize, of course, there isn't a thing we can do to get you out. Not a thing."

"Yes," said Johnny.

"You're a very brave man, or very much in love."

Hours later, the jet transport took off with Johnny in it.

He came down near what had been the border of the motherland and Poland. He began to walk. A farmer and his son spotted the parachute, came after him. The son was a Red Army man on leave. The son had a gun. He fired prematurely, and Johnny ran. It was hopeless, he decided. He would never make it. He would never even reach the capital alive, where they were holding Jo-Anne.

He ran.

He wished for rain. A blinding rainstorm. The clouds scudded in. The rain fell in buckets. The farmer and his son soon lost sight of Johnny.

Just to make sure, Johnny ran and let it go on raining.

"Floods in their motherland," the Secretary of Defense told the President. "Naturally, their news broadcasts are trying to keep the reports to a minimum, but these are the biggest floods we've ever heard of over there."

"Our man is there?" the President asked.

"He was dropped by parachute, sir!"

It was snowing when Johnny reached the capital. He had been parachuted into the enemy's motherland, naturally, because propinquity alone assured the success of his strange talent.

He was tired. His feet ached. He'd been the only one heading for the capital. Hundreds of thousands had been fleeing from the floods ...

"There he is!" a voice cried in the enemy language. He didn't understand the language, but he understood the tone. His picture had been flashed across the length and breadth of the motherland. He had been spotted.

He ran. Down an alley, across a muddy yard, floundering to his knees, then his thighs, in thick mud. They came floundering in pursuit. They fired a warning volley of shots. He stumbled and fell face down in the black, stinking mud.

They took him ...

Dark room. One light, on his face. A voice: "We can kill you."

"Kill me," he said. "My last wish will be for rain. Rain, forever."

"We can torture you."

"And I will say, before you start, let it rain and go on raining. Let me be powerless to prevent it. Rain!"

"We can kill the girl."

"Your country will float away."

A fist came at him out of the darkness. Hit him. It was tentative torture. He sobbed and thought: rain, harder. Rain, rain, rain ...

Water seeped into the dungeon. This had never happened before. The fist went away.

Outside it rained and rained.

"What does he want, comrade?"

"We don't know, comrade."

"Give it to him—whatever it is. He has disrupted our entire economy. We face economic disaster unless he—and his rain—leave us in peace."

"Perhaps that is what he wants. Peace."

"You fool! We are supposed to want peace. Shut up!"

"Yes, sir. Comrade."

"Better ask the party secretary."

"Yes, comrade."

The party secretary was asked. The party secretary sighed and nodded.

Johnny saw the light of day. And Jo-Anne.

A month later, the Secretary of Defense told him. "Thanks to you, they agreed to a German settlement, stopped sending arms to their Red ally in Asia, withdrew their promise of aid to the Arab fanatics, and have freed all foreigners held in their motherland illegally."

Johnny listened, smiling at Jo-Anne. They had been married two weeks. Naturally, the enemy had been only too glad to see them leave.

"Just stay available, Sloman," the President beamed from alongside the Secretary of Defense. "As long as they know we can always send you over there again, they'll never try anything. Right?"

"Yes, sir," said Johnny.

They called him the Weather Man. They went on calling him the Weather Man, although he retired more or less— except during cases of dire emergency.

The world called him that, the Weather Man. And, because he had retired to enjoy life with his new wife, they began to suspect, as could be expected, that he had been a fraud.

But the enemy did not think so. Ever again.

And that was enough for Johnny

THE NIGHT IS DARKENING ROUND ME

EMILY BRONTË

The night is darkening round me,
The wild winds coldly blow;
But a tyrant spell has bound me,
And I cannot, cannot go.

The giant trees are bending
Their bare boughs weighed with snow;
The storm is fast descending,
And yet I cannot go.

Clouds beyond clouds above me,
Wastes beyond wastes below;
But nothing drear can move me;
I will not, cannot go.

RAIN

EDWARD THOMAS

Rain, midnight rain, nothing but the wild rain
On this bleak hut, and solitude, and me
Remembering again that I shall die
And neither hear the rain nor give it thanks
For washing me cleaner than I have been
Since I was born into solitude.
Blessed are the dead that the rain rains upon:
But here I pray that none whom once I loved
Is dying tonight or lying still awake
Solitary, listening to the rain,
Either in pain or thus in sympathy
Helpless among the living and the dead,
Like a cold water among broken reeds,
Myriads of broken reeds all still and stiff,
Like me who have no love which this wild rain
Has not dissolved except the love of death,
If love it be towards what is perfect and
Cannot, the tempest tells me, disappoint.

RAIN

JEAN STARR UNTERMEYER

I have always hated the rain,
And the gloom of grayed skies.
But now I think I must always cherish
Rain-hung lead and the misty river;
And the friendly screen of dripping green
Where eager kisses were shyly give,
And your pipe-smoke made clouds in our damp, close
heaven.

The curious laggard passed us by,
His wet shoes soughed on the shining walk.
And that afternoon was filled with a blurred glory—
That afternoon, when we first talked as lovers.

THE STORM

ALAN L. STRANG

The rough old Mr. Storm
 Is whirling, swirling past
He makes the treetops bow their heads
 And trembles at his blast.

He never stops to think
 Of the damage he may do,
He's always rushing in and out
 And hitting, batting you.

He pushes big, black clouds
 Against the mountain tops;
The rain and hail comes rushing down
 In large, round crystal drops.

The storm will soon be over;
 See the rainbow in the sky.
The birds will sing on airy wing,
 And the bright sun shine on high.

STORM ENDING

JEAN TOOMER

Thunder blossoms gorgeously above our heads,
Great, hollow, bell-like flowers,
Rumbling in the wind,
Stretching clappers to strike our ears . . .
Full-lipped flowers
Bitten by the sun
Bleeding rain
Dripping rain like golden honey—
And the sweet earth flying from the thunder.

ABOUT THE TEAM

Madison Schmidt is the copy editor at Empire Press. She is the last roadblock for pesky errors when it comes to translating works from website to anthology print, as well as double checking front and back matter. When it comes to producing the Literary magazine, Madison works with our authors to finalize their writing for a perfect fit.

Madison is a Junior English major at the University of Nebraska-Lincoln and strives to be a copy editor in trade publishing upon graduation. She has taken multiple classes at the University in English and Journalism including both literature and writing courses. Madison also works with authors on goodreads.com to beta read fantasy and science fiction.

Melinda Frank is the marketing director at Empire Press. Her role is managing and developing all social media accounts for Empire Press. She is an English major with a psychology minor at the University of Nebraska-Lincoln. Melinda is a Senior that plans on pursuing a PhD in Ethnic Studies. She is originally from Los Angeles, California and has been able to travel and live in Tokyo, Hong Kong, and Shanghai. Melinda was drawn to Nebraska's writing program after attending the University of North Texas for her first two years of college.

During her time at UNL, Melinda has had the chance to intern for Prairie Schooner and the University of Nebraska Press. For Prairie Schooner, she had the chance to work with a team to review submissions for the magazine and work with senior editors to collaborate on new issues of the magazine. At the University of Nebraska Press, Melinda is a part of the acquisitions team and works with contracts, authors, and printing new books for the press. Melinda hopes to be a part of a publishing company that helps give a voice to those without one.

Brianna Patterson is the acquisitions editor for Empire Press. She is responsible for choosing the text and layout of the anthology and Literary magazine.

Brianna is a Junior English major at the University of Nebraska-Lincoln. She is from Omaha, Nebraska, but lives in Lincoln with her best friend and their dog, Cooper. Brianna currently works full time and Developmental Services of Nebraska-Lincoln, supporting individuals with disabilities. After graduating, Brianna wants to use her degree to pursue a career in editing and publishing as well as move to Washington State. She loves to travel and hopes she can venture outside the Midwest in the future. In Brianna's free time, she likes to write and read, hang out with friends and family, and play with her dog. She hopes to get more involved with different intern opportunities throughout the remainder of her time at UNL.

Alexa Horn is the designer at Empire Press. She is an advertising/public relations and journalism double-major at the University of Nebraska-Lincoln. She enjoys reading non-fiction, especially anything by Erik Larson, and playing video games. She is a Nebraska native, but it wasn't until recently that she began to appreciate the history and ecology of the Great Plains. She hopes to explore more of it in the future. She also wants to use her design skills to make anything except junk. There's a lot of extra stuff in this world, so she looks forward to creating something meaningful.